BADASS
POSITIVE AFFIRMATIONS
FOR MEN

BADASS
POSITIVE AFFIRMATIONS
FOR MEN

M NGAIHLIAN

For permission contact mngaihlian23@gmail.com

ISBN: 9798864117682
Imprint: Independently published

This book is dedicated to You.

So, here is to you – Live your life to your full potential!

Books By M Ngaihlian:

1. Living Beyond Regrets
2. What The Heck! Do It Anyway!
3. Living With Purpose And No Regrets
4. Does God Care About Me?
5. 120 Memory Verses For Kids
6. 3250+ Bible Verses For Every Day & Situation
7. Important Questions To Ask Yourself
8. Just Because You
9. I Am Affirmation Bible Verses For Girls
10. I Am Affirmation Bible Verses For Boys
11. I Am Affirmation Bible Verses For Women
12. I Am Affirmation Bible Verses For Men
13. Badass Positive Affirmations For Dads
14. Badass Positive Affirmations For Women
15. Badass Affirmations For Moms

INTRODUCTION

THE POWER OF POSITIVE AFFIRMATIONS

Affirmations are not mere self-talk or words. They tap into the intricate workings of your brain and your subconscious mind. When you consistently repeat positive affirmations, you are, in essence, rewiring your thought patterns. Your brain responds to these repetitive messages by creating new neural pathways, reinforcing positive beliefs, and challenging negative ones - unlocking your full potential and reshaping your life. They hold the power to transform your mindset, boost your self-confidence, and lead you on a path to personal growth and fulfillment.

Studies in neuroscience have shown that affirmations can stimulate the brain's reward centers, releasing dopamine—a neurotransmitter associated with pleasure and motivation. This creates a positive feedback loop, making you more likely to continue the affirmations and embrace the associated beliefs.

THE PSYCHOLOGY OF AFFIRMATIONS

Affirmations work because they operate on fundamental psychological principles. Here's how they can impact your mental and emotional well-being:

Boosting Self-Esteem:
Affirmations help counteract self-doubt and negative self-perception. By repeating positive statements about yourself, you gradually boost your self-esteem and self-worth.

Changing Negative Beliefs:
Often, we hold limiting beliefs about our capabilities or self-worth. Affirmations challenge these beliefs and encourage a more empowering perspective.

Shifting Focus:
Negative thoughts can dominate your mind and perpetuate a cycle of pessimism. Affirmations redirect your focus toward positive possibilities and opportunities.

Increasing Resilience:
Regular use of affirmations builds emotional resilience. You become better equipped to handle challenges, setbacks, and stress with a positive outlook.

Cultivating a Growth Mindset:
Affirmations foster a growth mindset—a belief that your abilities and intelligence can be developed through effort and learning. This mindset drives you to seek self-improvement.

HOW TO MANIFEST YOUR AFFIRMATIONS

Making affirmations work effectively involves more than just repeating positive statements; it requires a strategic and mindful approach. To harness the power of positive affirmations effectively, consider these practical strategies:

Set Clear Goals:
Begin with a clear understanding of what you want to achieve. Define your goals and intentions. Affirmations are most powerful when they are aligned with specific objectives.

Choose Affirmations Wisely:
Select affirmations that resonate with your goals and values. Ensure they are positive, present tense, and achievable.

Be Specific:
Focus on specific areas of your life or qualities you want to improve. Generic affirmations may not have the same impact as targeted ones.

Use Present Tense:
Phrase your affirmations in the present tense as if you're already experiencing the desired outcome. For example, say, "I am confident" rather than "I will be confident."

Customize:
Tailor affirmations to your unique goals and desires. Personalize them so they resonate deeply with your aspirations.

Repeat Consistently:
Consistency is key. Incorporate affirmations into your daily routine—morning, noon, and night—to reinforce positive beliefs.

Practice Patience:
Positive changes take time. Be patient with yourself. It may take weeks or even months to see significant results. Trust the process and remain committed.

Combine with Action:
While affirmations can influence your mindset, they work best when combined with action. Take steps, no matter how small, toward your goals. Action reinforces belief in your affirmations.

Believe in Them:
To make affirmations work, you must genuinely believe in them. If you encounter resistance or skepticism, address those doubts. Provide evidence and examples that support the affirmations.

Eliminate Negative Self-Talk:
Pay attention to your inner dialogue and replace self-criticism with affirmations. When you catch yourself thinking negatively, counteract it with a positive affirmation.

Journal Your Progress:
Keep a journal to record your experiences and observations. Track any shifts in your mindset, behavior, or circumstances. Documenting your progress helps reinforce the effectiveness of affirmations.

Use Emotion and Visualization:
As you repeat affirmations, engage your emotions and imagination. Feel the emotions associated with the affirmations. Visualize yourself living the reality described in the statements. This emotional and visual connection makes affirmations more potent.

Surround Yourself with Positivity:
Create an environment that supports your affirmations. Surround yourself with positive people, motivational quotes, and images that align with your goals.

Stay Open to Opportunities:
Be receptive to opportunities that align with your affirmations. Act on these opportunities when they arise. Affirmations can guide your actions and decisions.

Seek Accountability and Support:
Share your affirmations and goals with a trusted friend, mentor, or coach. They can provide support, and encouragement, and hold you accountable.

Adapt and Evolve:
As you make progress, revisit your affirmations regularly. Adjust them to reflect your evolving goals and beliefs. Growth and change are natural, so adapt your affirmations accordingly.

Live the Affirmations:
Ultimately, affirmations work when you integrate their messages into your daily life. Let them guide your actions, decisions, and interactions. Live as if you've already embraced the positive beliefs they convey.

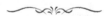

HOW TO USE THIS BOOK

1. Start with an Open Mind
Before you dive into the affirmations, approach this book with an open mind. Be willing to explore new ideas, challenge your existing beliefs, and embrace the potential for positive change in your life.

2. Set Clear Intentions
Begin by setting clear intentions for what you hope to achieve by using this book. What areas of your life do you want to improve? What specific goals do you want to work towards? Having a clear purpose will guide your journey.

3. Daily Affirmation Practice
The heart of this book lies in its affirmations. Each affirmation is a statement of empowerment, designed to reshape your mindset and boost your confidence. Incorporate these affirmations into your daily routine.

Morning Routine: Start your day by reading and reflecting on one or more affirmations. This will set a positive tone for the day ahead.

Throughout the Day: Carry a few affirmations with you on a small card or note in your pocket or wallet. Whenever you have a moment, revisit these affirmations to reinforce their messages.

Before Bed: End your day by revisiting the affirmations. Reflect on your experiences and how the affirmations impacted your thoughts and actions during the day.

4. Visualization
As you read and recite the affirmations, take a moment to visualize the positive outcomes they describe. Imagine yourself living the life you desire, achieving your goals, and embodying the qualities mentioned in the affirmations. Visualization adds depth and emotional connection to the process.

5. Journaling
Consider keeping a journal to record your experiences and reflections as you work with the affirmations. Write down any shifts in your mindset, any positive changes in your behavior, and any challenges you encounter. Journaling provides a valuable record of your progress.

6. Be Consistent
Consistency is crucial for the effectiveness of affirmations. Make a commitment to practice daily, even on days when you might not feel your best. Over time, the affirmations will become ingrained in your thinking.

7. Adapt and Customize
Feel free to adapt the affirmations to your specific goals and needs. You can modify them to make them more personal and relevant to your life. The key is to make them resonate with you on a deep level.

Affirmations are not just words but the embodiment of your inner potential. As you embrace their power, you will unlock the incredible capacity within you to create the life you desire—one empowered belief at a time. It's time to transform your mind and, in doing so, transform your life.

1

"I AM A BADASS, AND I OWN IT!"

Being a badass means being confident, assertive, and unapologetically yourself. When you own your badassery, you embrace your unique qualities, strengths, and quirks. It's about being fearless in pursuing your goals and dreams, standing up for what you believe in, and not letting anyone or anything hold you back.

When you own your badassery, you exude self-assuredness and authenticity. You're not swayed by others' opinions, and you confidently pursue your goals.

2

"I AM A BEACON
OF HOPE IN TIMES OF DESPAIR"

Being a beacon of hope means providing inspiration and optimism to those around you, especially during difficult times. It's about offering support, encouragement, and a positive outlook when others may be feeling lost or hopeless. By embodying this role, you become a source of light and guidance, helping people find their way through darkness and adversity.

3

"I AM A BEACON OF LIGHT IN THE DARKNESS"

Being a beacon of light signifies your ability to shine brightly even in the darkest of circumstances. It means spreading positivity, kindness, and warmth to dispel negativity and gloom. This affirmation reminds you that you have the power to bring light and joy to others' lives and make the world a better place.

4

"I AM A BEACON
OF INSPIRATION AND CREATIVITY"

Embracing your role as a beacon of inspiration and creativity means recognizing your potential to spark innovative ideas and motivate others to pursue their passions. Creativity is a powerful force that can drive positive change and transform the world. By being an inspiration to those around you, you encourage them to tap into their creative potential and make a difference in their own unique ways.

5

"I AM A BEACON OF POSITIVITY AND OPTIMISM"

Positivity and optimism are like a ray of sunshine in the darkest of times. When you embody these qualities, you inspire those around you to see the silver lining in any situation. Your positive outlook becomes contagious, creating an atmosphere of hope and resilience.

6

"I AM A BEACON
OF STRENGTH AND RESILIENCE"

Life is filled with ups and downs, but being a beacon of strength and resilience means that you can weather any storm that comes your way. You acknowledge your inner power and determination to bounce back from adversity. Your strength inspires others to tap into their resilience and face their own challenges with unwavering resolve.

7

"I AM A BEACON OF EMPATHY AND UNDERSTANDING"

Empathy is a remarkable quality that allows you to connect with and understand the emotions of others. When you embody this affirmation, you become a source of comfort and support for those who need it. Your ability to listen, empathize, and offer understanding helps foster deeper connections and promotes emotional well-being in your relationships.

8

"I AM A BELIEVER IN MY DREAMS"

Believing in your dreams is the first step toward achieving them. This affirmation reminds you of your unwavering faith in your goals and aspirations. It's about trusting in your abilities and working tirelessly to turn your dreams into reality. Your belief in yourself serves as the driving force behind your pursuit of success.

9

"I AM A BUILDER OF DREAMS AND ASPIRATIONS"

Not only do you believe in your own dreams, but you also actively work to build and nurture them. This means setting clear goals, creating plans, and taking action to turn your aspirations into tangible accomplishments. By being a builder of dreams, you demonstrate the importance of dedication and perseverance in achieving your objectives.

10

"I AM A BEACON OF CONFIDENCE AND SELF-ASSUREDNESS"

Confidence is a powerful trait that attracts success. When you carry yourself with confidence and self-assuredness, you project an aura of capability and competence. This not only boosts your own self-esteem but also inspires confidence in others' belief in you.

11

"I AM A BELIEVER IN MY OWN POTENTIAL"

Acknowledging your potential is essential for personal growth and self-development. When you believe in your own potential, you recognize that you have the capacity to learn, adapt, and achieve greatness. This mindset empowers you to step outside your comfort zone, take on new challenges, and reach heights you may have never imagined.

12

"I AM A BUILDER OF BRIDGES, NOT WALLS"

Building bridges is a metaphor for fostering connections, understanding, and cooperation with others. This affirmation emphasizes your commitment to inclusivity, collaboration, and open communication. It encourages you to seek common ground and find solutions that unite people rather than create divisions or barriers.

13

"I AM A CATALYST FOR POSITIVE TRANSFORMATION"

Being a catalyst for positive transformation means inspiring and driving change for the better. You recognize your role in initiating and supporting positive shifts in various aspects of life, whether it's personal growth, community improvement, or societal progress. Your actions and influence motivate others to join in the journey toward positive change.

14

"I AM A CHAMPION, ALWAYS STRIVING FOR GREATNESS"

Being a champion means consistently pushing your limits and aiming for excellence. You don't settle for mediocrity; you aspire to be the best version of yourself. Your pursuit of greatness becomes an inspiration to others on their own journeys of self-improvement.

15

"I AM A CONSTANT SOURCE OF MOTIVATION FOR MYSELF"

Self-motivation is key to achieving personal success. When you're a constant source of motivation for yourself, you're not reliant on external factors to keep you going. This inner drive propels you forward, setting an example for others to find their own inner motivation.

16

"I AM A CATALYST FOR CHANGE AND PROGRESS"

As a catalyst for change, you initiate positive transformations. Your innovative ideas and willingness to embrace change encourage those around you to adapt, evolve, and grow. Your actions become a driving force for progress.

17

"I AM A FEARLESS EXPLORER OF MY POTENTIAL"

Exploring your potential means stepping out of your comfort zone and taking on new challenges. When you fearlessly explore your capabilities, you inspire others to do the same. Your journey becomes a testament to the boundless potential within each individual.

18

"I AM A FORCE TO BE RECKONED WITH"

Being a force to be reckoned with implies strength and determination. You are unyielding in your pursuit of goals and unafraid to tackle challenges head-on. Others recognize your resilience and determination, making you a role model for perseverance.

19

"I AM A CHAMPION OF EMPOWERMENT"

Empowerment involves helping others recognize their strengths and potential, enabling them to take control of their lives. You are dedicated to uplifting and supporting those around you, empowering them to overcome challenges and achieve their goals. Your encouragement and belief in their abilities inspire them to pursue their dreams with confidence.

20

"I AM A CREATOR OF MY OWN REALITY"

Your reality is shaped by your thoughts, beliefs, and actions. This affirmation emphasizes your role as the architect of your own experiences. It encourages you to cultivate a positive mindset, make conscious choices, and take responsibility for the outcomes in your life. By doing so, you create a reality that aligns with your desires and values.

21

"I AM A FEARLESS EXPLORER OF LIFE'S ADVENTURES"

Life is an incredible journey filled with opportunities and experiences. As a fearless explorer of life's adventures, you embrace each moment with curiosity and enthusiasm. Your willingness to take risks and explore the unknown inspires others to live life to the fullest, encouraging them to step out of their comfort zones and create memorable experiences.

22

"I AM A CREATOR OF CHANGE AND TRANSFORMATION"

Change is a natural part of life, and you embrace it as an opportunity for growth and transformation. This affirmation signifies your role as a change-maker, actively seeking positive changes in your life and the world around you. Your willingness to adapt and evolve sets an example for others to follow.

23

"I AM A CONQUEROR OF FEAR AND DOUBT"

Fear and doubt can be formidable obstacles, but you refuse to let them control your actions and decisions. This affirmation reflects your courage and determination to confront and conquer these inner challenges. You recognize that fear and doubt are natural emotions, but they do not define your potential or limit your achievements.

24

"I AM A CREATOR OF JOY AND HAPPINESS"

Bringing joy and happiness into your life and the lives of others is a noble pursuit. This affirmation highlights your commitment to fostering positivity and spreading happiness through your actions, words, and attitude. Your infectious enthusiasm and uplifting presence brighten the days of those around you.

25

"I AM A GIVER, ALWAYS WILLING TO LEND A HELPING HAND"

Generosity is a noble trait that fosters positive connections and a sense of community. When you are a giver, you offer your support, time, and resources to those in need. Your willingness to lend a helping hand not only benefits others but also creates a ripple effect of kindness and compassion in the world.

26

"I AM A LEADER, AND OTHERS LOOK UP TO ME"

Leadership is about setting an example and inspiring others to follow your lead. When you are a leader, people naturally look up to you for guidance and direction. Your actions and decisions serve as a source of inspiration, motivating others to achieve their own potential and become leaders themselves.

27

"I AM A LEADER WHO EMPOWERS THOSE AROUND ME"

True leadership is not about control but about empowering others to reach their full potential. You create an environment where people feel valued, heard, and capable of making a difference. Your leadership style fosters a sense of ownership and responsibility in others, helping them grow and excel.

28

"I AM A FORCE TO BE RECKONED WITH"

Being a force to be reckoned with suggests that you are a formidable presence in any situation. You approach challenges with confidence and determination, knowing that you have the strength and capability to overcome them. This mindset empowers you to face adversity head-on and achieve your goals.

29

"I AM A FORCE OF NATURE, UNSTOPPABLE AND UNYIELDING"

Nature is a powerful and relentless force, and this affirmation compares your determination and resilience to the forces of nature. It signifies your unwavering commitment to your goals and your refusal to give in to obstacles or setbacks. You forge ahead with unstoppable determination.

30

"I AM A FORCE FOR POSITIVE CHANGE"

As a force for positive change, you actively work to make the world a better place. This affirmation emphasizes your role in creating solutions, inspiring others, and driving progress in your community and beyond. Your actions serve as a catalyst for meaningful and lasting change.

31

"I AM A FIGHTER, NOT A VICTIM"

This affirmation reinforces your warrior spirit and determination to face life's challenges head-on. It signifies your refusal to adopt a victim mentality, even in the face of adversity. Instead, you choose to fight for what you believe in and overcome obstacles with strength and resilience.

32

"I AM A FEARLESS EXPLORER OF LIFE"

Life is an adventure, and you approach it fearlessly, eager to explore its many facets and opportunities. This affirmation highlights your adventurous spirit, curiosity, and willingness to embrace the unknown. Your fearlessness leads to personal growth and enriching experiences.

33

"I AM A GAME-CHANGER"

Being a game-changer means having the ability to disrupt the status quo and make a significant impact on your chosen path. This affirmation reflects your determination to innovate, challenge conventions, and lead the way in your endeavors. You aspire to leave a lasting mark on the world.

34

"I AM A HARBINGER OF PEACE AND HARMONY"

Promoting peace and harmony is a noble mission, and this affirmation signifies your commitment to creating environments of tranquility and unity. You work to resolve conflicts, foster understanding, and bring people together. Your efforts contribute to a more peaceful and harmonious world.

35

"I AM A KEEPER OF PROMISES AND COMMITMENTS"

Keeping your promises and honoring your commitments is a sign of integrity and reliability. This affirmation highlights your dedication to upholding your word and following through on your obligations. Your trustworthiness strengthens your relationships and builds a reputation for dependability.

36

"I AM A LEADER WHO LEADS WITH LOVE"

Leadership rooted in love emphasizes empathy, compassion, and caring for the well-being of others. This affirmation reflects your leadership style, which prioritizes the emotional and personal growth of those you lead. Your leadership fosters a sense of belonging and support within your team.

37

"I AM A LEADER WHO LEADS WITH INTEGRITY"

Integrity is the cornerstone of effective leadership, and you lead by example in this regard. This affirmation underscores your commitment to honesty, ethics, and moral principles. You inspire trust and respect in your leadership, setting a standard of excellence for others to follow.

38

"I AM A LEADER WHO LEADS BY EXAMPLE"

Leading by example is one of the most effective forms of leadership. When you consistently demonstrate the qualities and values you expect from others, you earn their respect and trust. Your actions become a blueprint for how to navigate challenges and succeed with integrity.

39

"I AM A LEADER WHO LEADS WITH EMPATHY AND COMPASSION"

Effective leadership involves understanding and caring for the well-being of those you lead. When you lead with empathy and compassion, you create a supportive and nurturing environment. Your genuine concern for others fosters trust, cooperation, and a sense of belonging within your team or community.

40

"I AM A LEADER WHO INSPIRES OTHERS TO GREATNESS"

Great leaders inspire others to reach their full potential. Your vision, enthusiasm, and dedication motivate those around you to set higher goals and strive for excellence. Your ability to ignite a sense of purpose in others makes you a catalyst for personal and collective success.

41

"I AM A MAN OF CHARACTER AND INTEGRITY"

Character and integrity are the foundation of trust and respect. As a person of character, you consistently uphold moral and ethical principles. Your unwavering commitment to doing what is right sets a high standard for ethical behavior, influencing others to follow your example.

42

"I AM A MAGNET FOR SUCCESS AND ABUNDANCE"

This affirmation signifies your belief in the law of attraction —that by focusing on success and abundance, you draw these qualities into your life. Your mindset and actions align with your desire for achievement and prosperity, making you a magnet for opportunities and wealth.

43

"I AM A MAN OF COURAGE AND BRAVERY"

Courage is the willingness to face challenges and adversity with determination. As a man of courage and bravery, you confront obstacles head-on, inspiring others to confront their fears and pursue their goals fearlessly. Your resilience in the face of adversity is a source of inspiration for all.

44

"I AM A MANIFESTOR OF DREAMS AND DESIRES"

Manifestation is the act of turning your dreams and desires into reality through focused intention and action. This affirmation reflects your ability to manifest your goals by aligning your thoughts, beliefs, and actions with your aspirations. You recognize the power of visualization and positive thinking in achieving your dreams.

45

"I AM A MAN OF ACTION, NOT JUST WORDS"

Actions speak louder than words. When you are a man of action, you demonstrate your commitment to your goals and values through your deeds. Your ability to turn ideas into tangible results motivates others to take proactive steps toward their own aspirations.

46

"I AM A PROBLEM SOLVER"

Problem-solving is a crucial skill in life, and this affirmation underscores your ability to tackle challenges with a solution-oriented mindset. You approach problems with creativity, critical thinking, and determination, seeking to find effective resolutions. Your problem-solving skills make you a valuable asset in any situation.

47

"I AM A PIONEER OF INNOVATION AND PROGRESS"

Pioneering innovation and progress involves pushing boundaries and introducing new ideas and technologies. This affirmation reflects your role as an innovator, continuously seeking to improve and advance in your field. You inspire others to embrace change and strive for excellence.

48

"I AM A MAN OF HONOR, TRUE TO MY WORD"

Honor is a mark of integrity and reliability. When you are a man of honor, your word is your bond. Others can trust that you will follow through on your commitments, creating a sense of dependability and trustworthiness that enhances your relationships and reputation.

49

"I AM A MAN OF FAITH, BELIEVING IN MYSELF AND MY PATH"

Self-belief and faith in your journey are essential for personal growth and achievement. Your unwavering belief in yourself and your path encourages others to trust in their own abilities and embrace their unique journeys with confidence and determination.

50

"I AM A MAN OF SUBSTANCE AND DEPTH"

Substance and depth signify a rich and meaningful existence. As a person of substance and depth, you seek to understand life's complexities, dive deep into your interests, and engage in profound conversations. Your pursuit of depth inspires others to explore their passions and cultivate a deeper understanding of themselves and the world around them.

51

"I AM A SOURCE OF LOVE AND JOY"

Love and joy are powerful emotions that can uplift and transform lives. This affirmation signifies your role as a source of these positive emotions, both for yourself and for others. Your ability to spread love and joy creates a happier and more harmonious environment.

52

"I AM A SOURCE OF STRENGTH FOR MY LOVED ONES"

Your loved ones can find solace and support in your strength and presence. This affirmation reflects your role as a pillar of strength for those you care about. Your unwavering support and reliability bring comfort to those who turn to you in times of need.

53

"I AM A SOURCE OF STRENGTH AND SUPPORT"

Beyond your loved ones, you are also a source of strength and support for your community and beyond. This affirmation signifies your dedication to helping others and making a positive impact. Your willingness to lend a helping hand and offer support enriches the lives of many.

54

"I AM A SOURCE OF INSPIRATION FOR GENERATIONS TO COME"

Your actions and choices have the potential to inspire future generations. This affirmation underscores your role as a source of inspiration, leaving a lasting legacy of positive influence and motivation for those who follow in your footsteps.

55

"I AM A SEEKER OF KNOWLEDGE AND WISDOM"

Knowledge and wisdom are lifelong pursuits, and this affirmation reflects your commitment to continuous learning and personal growth. You seek knowledge and wisdom from various sources, recognizing that they are valuable tools for navigating life's complexities.

56

"I AM A SHINING EXAMPLE OF RESILIENCE"

Resilience is the ability to bounce back from adversity, and this affirmation signifies your capacity to weather life's storms with strength and grace. You serve as a shining example of resilience, inspiring others to face challenges with courage and resilience.

57

"I AM A SYMBOL
OF ENDURANCE AND FORTITUDE"

Endurance and fortitude are qualities that enable you to persist in the face of difficulty and hardship. This affirmation represents your determination to withstand adversity and keep moving forward. You embody the spirit of resilience and endurance, showing others that they can overcome even the toughest obstacles.

58

"I AM A TRAILBLAZER, NOT A FOLLOWER"

Being a trailblazer means forging your own path rather than following the crowd. This affirmation reflects your determination to lead by example, setting your own standards and paving the way for others to follow. You are unafraid to take risks and embrace innovation.

59

"I AM A TRAILBLAZER, FORGING MY OWN PATH"

This affirmation emphasizes your role as a pioneer, carving out a unique and distinctive journey through life. You are not bound by convention or tradition but instead, create your own destiny by following your passions and ambitions. Your trailblazing spirit inspires others to embrace their individuality.

60

"I AM A TRAILBLAZER, BREAKING NEW GROUND"

Breaking new ground involves pushing the boundaries of what is possible and challenging established norms. This affirmation signifies your commitment to innovation and progress. You actively seek opportunities to make a significant impact and leave a mark on the world.

61

"I AM A TRAILBLAZER, PAVING THE WAY FOR OTHERS"

As a trailblazer, you don't just pursue your own path—you also create opportunities and remove obstacles for those who come after you. This affirmation reflects your role as a mentor and guide, helping others find their way and achieve their aspirations.

62

"I AM A TORCHBEARER FOR POSITIVE CHANGE"

Being a torchbearer for positive change means carrying the light of progress and transformation into the world. This affirmation signifies your commitment to driving meaningful change in your community and society at large. You actively work to illuminate the path toward a brighter future.

63

"I AM A MAN OF AMBITION AND DRIVE"

Ambition and drive are the engines that propel you toward your goals. When you are a man of ambition and drive, you demonstrate an unwavering commitment to achieving your aspirations. Your relentless pursuit of success motivates others to set ambitious goals and pursue their dreams with determination.

64

"I AM A MAN OF VISION AND PURPOSE"

Vision and purpose provide direction and meaning to your life. When you are a man of vision and purpose, you have a clear sense of where you're going and why. Your commitment to your vision inspires others to discover their own life's purpose and work towards fulfilling it with passion and dedication.

65

"I AM A MASTER OF SELF-CONTROL"

Self-control is the ability to manage your impulses and emotions effectively. As a master of self-control, you demonstrate discipline in your actions and decisions. Your self-discipline serves as an example for others, encouraging them to develop greater self-control and make sound choices in their lives.

66

"I AM A WINNER, NOT A QUITTER"

Success often requires perseverance and determination, and this affirmation emphasizes your commitment to winning at life's challenges. You refuse to give up when faced with obstacles or setbacks. Instead, you view every challenge as an opportunity to learn and grow, ultimately leading to victory.

67

"I AM A WARRIOR, NOT A WORRIER"

Worry and anxiety can be paralyzing, but you choose to adopt a warrior mindset instead. This affirmation signifies your determination to face challenges with courage and resilience rather than succumbing to worry. You tackle problems head-on and approach them as opportunities for growth.

68

"I AM A WARRIOR
OF COURAGE AND BRAVERY"

Courage and bravery are essential qualities for facing adversity and overcoming fear. This affirmation signifies your warrior spirit, demonstrating your readiness to confront challenges head-on with courage and determination. Your bravery inspires others to summon their inner strength.

69

"I AM A TRUE GENTLEMAN, TREATING OTHERS WITH RESPECT"

Being a true gentleman involves treating others with courtesy, respect, and consideration. Your behavior sets an example of how to interact with kindness and respect, fostering harmonious relationships and encouraging others to practice these values as well.

70

"I AM A WARRIOR FOR JUSTICE AND EQUALITY"

Advocating for justice and equality is a noble cause. As a warrior for justice and equality, you stand up for what is right and work towards creating a fair and inclusive society. Your commitment to these principles inspires others to join the fight for a more just and equitable world.

71

"I AM A WINNER IN EVERY ASPECT OF LIFE"

Winning is not solely about victory in competitions but also about achieving success in various aspects of life. When you consider yourself a winner, you maintain a winning mindset, approaching challenges with confidence and determination, and encouraging others to do the same.

72

"I AM A WARRIOR OF POSITIVITY AND OPTIMISM"

Positivity and optimism are powerful forces for overcoming adversity and achieving success. This affirmation signifies your role as a warrior of these qualities, choosing to see the bright side of life and maintain a hopeful outlook. Your positivity is contagious and inspires others to adopt a similar mindset.

73

"I AM ALWAYS LEARNING AND GROWING"

Lifelong learning and personal growth are ongoing processes. As someone committed to always learning and growing, you set an example of continuous self-improvement. Your pursuit of knowledge and self-development inspires others to embrace a growth mindset and seek opportunities for learning and growth.

74

"I AM A WARRIOR OF HOPE AND POSITIVITY"

This affirmation reinforces your role as a warrior of hope and positivity, actively working to inspire optimism and confidence in others. Your determination to spread hope and positivity serves as a beacon of light in times of darkness, motivating those around you to keep pushing forward.

75

"I AM AN ADVOCATE FOR MAKING A POSITIVE IMPACT"

Advocating for positive impact means actively working to create a better world for yourself and others. This affirmation signifies your dedication to championing causes and initiatives that make a meaningful difference. Your advocacy inspires others to join you in creating positive change.

76

"I AM CONFIDENT IN MY ABILITIES AND TALENTS"

Confidence in your abilities and talents is a key factor in achieving your goals. Your self-assuredness encourages others to believe in their own abilities and pursue their passions with confidence.

77

"I AM AN ADVOCATE FOR CREATING A BETTER WORLD"

Creating a better world requires collective effort and a commitment to positive change. This affirmation signifies your role as an advocate for improving society, promoting justice, and fostering inclusivity. Your advocacy inspires others to join the mission of creating a more equitable and compassionate world.

78

"I AM AN ADVOCATE FOR LIVING LIFE TO THE FULLEST"

Life is a precious gift, and this affirmation reflects your advocacy for embracing every moment and living life to the fullest. You inspire others to pursue their passions, seek adventure, and make the most of their experiences. Your enthusiasm for life is contagious.

79

"I AM AN ADVOCATE FOR NEVER GIVING UP"

Giving up is not an option for those who are determined to achieve their goals. This affirmation signifies your role as an advocate for perseverance and resilience. You motivate others to keep pushing forward, even when faced with challenges, knowing that persistence leads to success.

80

"I AM CONSTANTLY GROWING AND EVOLVING"

Growth and evolution are continuous processes throughout life. This affirmation reflects your commitment to personal development and self-improvement. You embrace change and actively seek opportunities for growth, both in your skills and your understanding of the world.

81

"I AM FEARLESS IN PURSUING MY GOALS"

Fearlessness in pursuing your goals means you don't let fear or doubt hold you back. Your fearless approach to goal-setting motivates others to overcome their own fears and take bold steps toward their aspirations.

82

"I AM DETERMINED AND UNSTOPPABLE"

Determination and an unwavering spirit are the driving forces behind overcoming obstacles. As someone who is determined and unstoppable, you inspire others to persevere in the face of challenges, reminding them that determination can lead to triumph.

83

"I AM IN CONTROL OF MY DESTINY"

Taking control of your destiny means recognizing your power to shape your own life. This affirmation reflects your sense of agency and responsibility for your future. You make choices and take actions that align with your goals, actively steering your life in the direction you desire.

84

"I AM RESILIENT
IN THE FACE OF CHALLENGES"

Resilience is a vital quality for navigating life's difficulties. This affirmation signifies your capacity to bounce back from setbacks and adapt to adversity with strength and determination. Your resilience serves as a source of inspiration for others facing their own challenges.

85

"I AM STRONG AND CAPABLE"

Strength and capability are assets that empower you to overcome obstacles and achieve your goals. This affirmation reflects your recognition of your inner strength and competence. You approach tasks and challenges with confidence, knowing that you are capable of success.

86

"I AM THE ARCHITECT OF MY OWN SUCCESS"

Success is not a matter of chance but a result of deliberate actions and choices. This affirmation signifies your role as the architect of your own success. You set goals, make plans, and take consistent steps toward achieving your aspirations.

87

"I AM THE CAPTAIN OF MY SHIP"

Taking control of your life means recognizing yourself as the captain of your own ship, steering it in the direction you desire. This affirmation emphasizes your role as the leader of your own journey, responsible for making choices and navigating the course of your life.

88

"I AM DISCIPLINED AND DEDICATED TO MY GOALS"

Discipline and dedication are essential for achieving long-term success. Your disciplined approach to goal pursuit serves as a model for others, illustrating the value of consistency and hard work in attaining one's objectives.

89

"I AM FOCUSED ON WHAT TRULY MATTERS IN LIFE"

Focus on what truly matters means prioritizing your values and what brings you fulfillment. Your focus on what's important inspires others to reflect on their own priorities and make meaningful choices in life.

90

"I AM UNAPOLOGETICALLY MYSELF"

Being unapologetically yourself means embracing your authenticity without reservation. This affirmation reflects your commitment to living in alignment with your true self, unburdened by societal pressures or the need for validation from others. You inspire others to do the same by your example.

91

"I AM UNSTOPPABLE IN MY PURSUIT OF HAPPINESS"

Happiness is a worthy pursuit, and this affirmation signifies your determination to achieve it. You view obstacles as opportunities for growth and strive relentlessly to create a life that brings you joy. Your pursuit of happiness inspires others to prioritize their own well-being.

92

"I AM WORTHY OF LOVE AND RESPECT"

Recognizing your own worth is essential for healthy self-esteem and relationships. This affirmation signifies your belief in your inherent worthiness of love and respect. You set boundaries and expect to be treated with kindness and consideration, inspiring others to do the same.

93

"I EMBRACE MY UNIQUENESS"

Embracing your uniqueness means celebrating your individuality and recognizing that it is a source of strength. This affirmation reflects your acceptance of your distinct qualities and encourages others to do the same. Your authenticity serves as an example for others to embrace their own uniqueness.

94

"I EMBRACE EVERY CHALLENGE AS AN OPPORTUNITY"

Challenges are not setbacks but opportunities for growth and learning. This affirmation signifies your readiness to face challenges with a positive and open mindset. You inspire others to view obstacles as stepping stones toward personal development and success.

95

"I EMBRACE VULNERABILITY AS A SOURCE OF STRENGTH"

Vulnerability is a powerful tool for building authentic connections and fostering empathy. This affirmation reflects your willingness to embrace vulnerability as a source of strength, both in your own life and in your relationships with others. Your vulnerability inspires trust and deepens your connections.

96

"I FEARLESSLY CHASE MY DREAMS"

Pursuing your dreams requires courage and determination, and this affirmation signifies your fearless pursuit of your aspirations. You are unafraid to chase your dreams, even when faced with uncertainty or setbacks. Your determination to follow your passions inspires others to do the same.

97

"I AM IN CHARGE OF MY OWN HAPPINESS"

Happiness is a choice, and taking charge of your own happiness means not relying on external circumstances for fulfillment. Your pursuit of happiness serves as a reminder to others that they have the power to cultivate joy and contentment in their lives.

98

"I STAND UP
FOR WHAT I BELIEVE IN"

Taking a stand for your beliefs is a sign of conviction and integrity. This affirmation signifies your commitment to speaking up and advocating for what you believe in, even in the face of opposition. Your willingness to stand up for your principles inspires others to do the same.

99

"I TRUST MY INSTINCTS AND MAKE WISE DECISIONS"

Trusting your instincts and making wise decisions come from self-awareness and experience. Your ability to trust your intuition and make sound choices guides others in developing their decision-making skills and honing their instincts.

100

"I AM A SEEKER OF TRUTH AND KNOWLEDGE"

This affirmation reflects your commitment to intellectual curiosity and the pursuit of truth. You understand that knowledge is a powerful tool for personal and societal progress, and you actively seek out opportunities for learning and growth. Your quest for truth and knowledge enriches your life and the lives of those around you.

101

"I AM A FIERCE ADVOCATE FOR MY OWN WELL-BEING"

Advocating for your own well-being means prioritizing self-care, setting boundaries, and making choices that promote your physical and mental health. It's about recognizing that you are your best advocate when it comes to taking care of yourself. This affirmation encourages self-empowerment, reminding you that you have the power and responsibility to protect and nurture your own well-being. It's about knowing when to say no, seeking help when needed, and making decisions that align with your health and happiness.

102

"I AM RESILIENT AND BOUNCE BACK FROM SETBACKS"

Resilience is the ability to adapt and recover from adversity. Your resilience in the face of setbacks inspires others to embrace challenges as opportunities for growth and learn to bounce back from life's setbacks.

103

"I AM COMFORTABLE IN MY OWN SKIN"

Being comfortable in your own skin means feeling at ease with who you are, without the need for external validation. It's about embracing your imperfections and celebrating your individuality. This affirmation encourages self-acceptance, allowing you to navigate life with confidence and authenticity. When you're comfortable in your own skin, you're better equipped to face challenges and pursue your dreams without the burden of self-doubt.

104

"I TRUST MYSELF TO MAKE THE RIGHT DECISIONS"

Trusting your own judgment is essential for personal growth and decision-making. It's a reminder that you possess the wisdom and intuition to navigate life's choices. This affirmation fosters self-confidence and resilience, as it encourages you to rely on your own insights and values when faced with decisions, big or small. Trusting yourself empowers you to take risks and learn from both successes and failures.

105

"I TRUST THE TIMING OF MY LIFE'S JOURNEY"

Patience is a virtue, and this affirmation reinforces the belief that everything happens in its own time. It's a reminder to have faith in the unfolding of your life's path, even when faced with setbacks or delays. Trusting the timing of your journey can reduce stress and anxiety, allowing you to embrace the present moment and focus on personal growth rather than constantly chasing future goals.

106

"I AM A LOVING AND SUPPORTIVE PARTNER"

This affirmation is not limited to romantic relationships but extends to all interactions. It underscores the importance of being caring, empathetic, and encouraging in your relationships. Being a loving and supportive partner means actively listening, providing emotional support, and nurturing the bonds you share with others. It also reflects your commitment to fostering healthy and positive connections in your life.

107

"I AM SURROUNDED BY LOVE AND POSITIVITY"

Your environment plays a significant role in your well-being. This affirmation acknowledges the power of positive surroundings and relationships. When you believe you are surrounded by love and positivity, you are more likely to attract and cultivate these qualities in your life. It encourages you to seek out positive influences and maintain boundaries with negative ones, creating a nurturing atmosphere that supports your growth and happiness.

108

"I AM WORTHY OF SUCCESS AND PROSPERITY"

Self-worth is the foundation of achievement. This affirmation reinforces the belief that you deserve success and prosperity in all areas of your life. It's a declaration that you are capable and deserving of achieving your goals and dreams. When you embrace this affirmation, you are more likely to pursue your ambitions with confidence and determination, overcoming self-doubt and fear of failure.

109

"I AM A MAGNET FOR HEALTHY AND LOVING RELATIONSHIPS"

Healthy relationships are essential for personal growth and well-being. This affirmation highlights your ability to attract and maintain relationships that are based on mutual respect, trust, and love. It encourages you to set high standards for your relationships, recognizing that you deserve nothing less than positivity and support in your connections with others.

110

"I AM RESILIENT AND UNBREAKABLE"

Resilience is the ability to bounce back from adversity and challenges. This affirmation reinforces your inner strength and determination. It reminds you that you can face difficulties with courage and adaptability, emerging stronger from life's trials. When you believe in your resilience, setbacks become opportunities for growth, and you develop the confidence to overcome obstacles.

"I AM UNAFRAID TO TAKE RISKS AND SEIZE OPPORTUNITIES"

Life is full of risks and opportunities, and embracing them requires courage. Your willingness to take risks and seize opportunities serves as an example for others to step outside their comfort zones and pursue their ambitions fearlessly.

112

"I AM CAPABLE OF ACHIEVING MY GOALS"

Believing in your ability to achieve your goals is a powerful motivator. This affirmation reinforces your determination to pursue your aspirations. It's a statement of self-belief that propels you forward, helping you set clear objectives, make plans, and work diligently to attain your dreams. When you internalize this affirmation, you develop a growth mindset that fuels your ambition.

113

"I AM A SOURCE OF HUMILITY AND MODESTY"

Humility and modesty are virtues that remind us to stay grounded and appreciative of our blessings. As a source of humility and modesty, you model the importance of acknowledging your strengths and accomplishments while remaining humble. Your demeanor encourages others to cultivate a sense of gratitude and humility in their own lives.

114

"I AM ALWAYS MOVING TOWARDS MY BEST SELF"

Self-improvement is an ongoing journey. This affirmation reflects your commitment to personal growth and development. It signifies your dedication to becoming the best version of yourself, both in terms of character and achievements. When you acknowledge that you are continually evolving, you stay motivated to make positive changes in your life.

115

"I AM THE AUTHOR OF MY OWN STORY"

This affirmation empowers you to take control of your life and make choices that align with your values and desires. It signifies that you have the power to shape your own narrative, overcome challenges, and create the future you envision. By embracing authorship of your story, you become the active agent of your life's journey.

116

"I AM WORTHY OF ALL THE GOOD THINGS LIFE HAS TO OFFER"

Self-worth and self-deservingness are at the core of this affirmation. It emphasizes that you are deserving of happiness, love, success, and all the positive experiences that life can offer. When you internalize this belief, you are more likely to pursue opportunities and make choices that align with your highest potential.

"MY VOICE MATTERS, AND I USE IT WITH COURAGE"

Your voice is a powerful tool for self-expression and advocating for what you believe in. This affirmation encourages you to speak up, share your thoughts, and stand up for your values. It reminds you that your perspective is valuable and that you have the courage to make a positive impact through your words and actions.

118

"I AM A SOURCE OF GRATITUDE AND APPRECIATION"

Expressing gratitude and appreciation fosters positivity and gratitude in others. As a source of gratitude and appreciation, you acknowledge and value the contributions and kindness of those around you. Your appreciation inspires others to recognize and express gratitude for the goodness in their lives.

119

"I AM A SOURCE OF FINANCIAL RESPONSIBILITY"

Responsible financial management is essential for long-term stability and security. As a source of financial responsibility, you make prudent financial choices and prioritize saving and investing wisely. Your financial discipline encourages others to take control of their finances and make informed money-related decisions.

120

"I AM A SOURCE OF OPEN-MINDEDNESS AND TOLERANCE"

Embracing diversity of thought and perspective promotes open-mindedness and tolerance. As a source of open-mindedness and tolerance, you actively listen to differing viewpoints and respect individual beliefs and opinions. Your open-mindedness fosters a climate of acceptance and encourages others to engage in constructive dialogue.

121

"MY POTENTIAL IS LIMITLESS"

This affirmation underscores the boundless nature of your potential. You recognize that there are no limits to what you can achieve and aspire to continually push the boundaries of your capabilities. Your belief in limitless potential serves as an inspiration for others to reach for their own highest aspirations.

These affirmations are a powerful reminder of your strength, resilience, and potential. Embrace them daily, and let them serve as a source of motivation and empowerment on your journey to becoming the best version of yourself. You are capable of achieving greatness, and the world is waiting for you to shine your light.

So... Go ahead...
Be *that* Badass Man You Were Meant To Be!

About The Author:

M Ngaihlian is a nurse by profession and a mother of two beautiful angels. Her passion for writing rekindles as she re-dedicated her life to be a voice, a shoulder to cry on, a helping hand for those downtrodden, outcast, and ignored people in society, and proclaim the love of God and His unfailing mercy and grace. She can be found online at pourbin.com.

Made in the USA
Monee, IL
14 December 2024